THE AMERICAN POETRY SERIES

Dennis Schmitz

Goodwill, Inc.

The Ecco Press 1975

First published in 1976 by The Ecco Press
1 West 30th Street, New York, N.Y. 10001
Published simultaneously in Canada by
The Macmillan Company of Canada Limited
Printed in U.S.A.

Designed by Ronald Gordon
The Ecco Press logo is by Ahmed Yacoubi

Library of Congress Cataloging in Publication Data
Schmitz, Dennis, 1937–
   Goodwill, Inc.
   (The American poetry series; v. 7)
   I. Title.
PS3569.C517G6   811'.5'4   75-25791
ISBN 0-912-94624-5

The publication of this book is partially
supported by a grant from
The National Endowment for the Arts

Grateful acknowledgment is made to the following
magazines in which some of these poems first appeared:

Antaeus: "Poke-Pole Fishing" and "Widow."
Chicago Review: "The Chalk Angel."
Cutbank: "Self-Portrait."
Epoch: "Monstrous Pictures of Whales."
Field: "Chicago: Near West-Side Renewal," "The Mole,"
portion of "The Name of Our Country," "Star & Garter
Theater," "Queen of Heaven Mausoleum," "Bathing in Dead
Man Creek," and "Building Marriage."
Iowa Review: "Goodwill, Inc."
Ironwood: Portion of "The California Phrasebook."
Lillabulero: "Allergy."
The North American Review: "The Name of Our Country."
The Paris Review: "Tattoo Artist."
Poetry Now: "Geography" and "The Day the Paint Factory
Burned."
Quarry: "To the Reader."
Stand: "For Elizabeth . . . ," portion of "The California
Phrasebook."
TriQuarterly: "First Snow."

For Loretta

Contents

Geography

Goodwill, Inc.

To The Reader

if only my tongue
were a latch in the mouth of love
& the used breath were not so thread-
bare I could warm your cold body
I could let you in for a rest
from your face opaque as an eyelid
over sorrow's parched dawn
wash your foreign body in the damp
remains of my own . . .

Chicago

Chicago: Near West-Side Renewal

sleep was only a dream
Death had of us
I am afraid to touch
the wall that might be
too warm
the house that bore its gifts
through the night
till the wet sun lapped at the windows

what is the good news I should send
of the sealed landscapes, corners
remembered by light—
yesterday's body has traveled
over the same bones to the older
man who crawls

his young belly bare against the rug
he raises a hand suddenly dipped
in the sun's fresh golden
spoor who tried to wake only
in the empty lots, to recover his own
spoor before he woke

too late! the roads lick up
every kind of weather. inside my breath
returned, a tired rider,
hunter, wet with the sweat of his beast.
before the keyhole's half-
lit eye the humid dreams drift like
flawed glass showing the night

we dimly saw, the common death that
stirred under the small crown
of the gas-ring, the domestic sadness
in the wallpaper's distant
foliage. at night a man discards
the daytime face, the flat
map of his globular, primitive heart
he is at home & loneliness is the local
weather.

all night long we built this house
body by body
because after the flesh spreads
its natural foliage
after our roots will only pull
up pain & we refer
to ourselves in the plural
your bitterness becomes my bitterness

& it is not enough to nail
a wife in Sunday
love or if you are a woman drive
your teeth again & again

into the walls of widowhood
instead you are a day-laborer
the Housing Authority hires
rural white, Southern black, planting

enormous blisters in the palms
you press to the old
walls papered with flowers rippling
under the wrecking ball's rusty sun
the bricks, worm-riddled joists
spineless linoleum & lintels
by which the living left
unused lengths of body preserved

in a permanent coat of fever:
this is our neighborhood broken
breath by breath
from our fathers. forty feet above
the broached foundation
only plumbing holds the bathroom
walls painted with the names
of the wrong loves, initials in the hearts
the graffiti a visitor
the lover who was a guest leaves.

The Chalk Angel

even though he falls
across it, not the drunk's

outline, nor the dog's
who drifts in
& out of the shape

scenting meat.
this is not what the child
was assigned who copied

the figure with stolen
schoolroom chalk.
tomorrow his teacher

too might have
used it for a math
problem: a measurement

of astral bodies.

The Day the Paint Factory Burned

exploded foreign tints: Florida
Evenglo or Hawaii
Sunset tattoo our slum
walls & up the street outline

against the fence a ravaged
Cadillac on blocks.
in it my two small daughters drive
out of their neighborhood

stalled lives. on its crazed
windshield the spider
legs of suburban streets
crawl the landscape

into their heads.
instead of khaki skies
the glass runs with
all they've ever dreamed—

no doll smeared with a kiss's
red focus, nor this world
uneven dark fills as the childhood
colors drain.

Goodwill, Inc.

caught at hanger's ends the limp
trousers suspended
from zippers like fish surprised
at what they carried
a king's ring or the genitals
that float like the air bladders
behind the fish's gills & take life
from the liquid where an alien heavy-

bodied animal may drown.
the belts, brassieres & galluses
with their elastic gone
in the orbits the bodies pulled
apart as they circled

each other. the big woman's
girdle broken
by buttocks that moved
like moons around her sex
till she strips
at night to that dark
reflected light a husband

sheds as he travels

in her stunning gravity.
Love, against your bin of odd
sizes I leaned last—
broken shoes, the borrowed old
man's digestion of a dead
wife who still travels the seamless
loneliness of his insides, or
that first love like a rare food
which went to fat about his loins.

in the dirty changing-room men &
women must share I assume other
men's clothes, as many as I can put
on of ever-larger sizes
till I stumble & weave

other richer lives on my own.

Star & Garter Theater

for Roger Aplon

it is always night here
faces close but never heal
only the eyes develop

scabs when we sleep & head
by head the dream is drained
into the white pool

of the screen. we go on rehearsing
THE REVENGE OF FRANKENSTEIN:
my arm is sewn to your shoulder.
your father's awful hand
& an actual criminal brain

take root under the projector's
cold moon. I wanted to do
only good. I planted my mouth
& kisses grew all over skid row.
now the fat ladies of the night

are lowered into the lace
stockings & strapped into their black
apparatus. this body is grafted
to theirs. alone we are helpless,

but put together winos, whores
& ambivalent dead we walk the daytime
world charged with our beauty.

The Mole

last of the poets, first of the undead
you must pound a pencil through his heart
before he bites the little seamstress
or gives her life eternal—

a poem patched together from calendars.
he detours through graves to kiss
our necks & nests in the intestines'

narrow tunnels: a penniless noble
without even a shadow to wear
out like the second in a two-
pants suit. how do I stop burrowing

into myself according to the legend,
blind. if I am dead I will be buried
with my toes around my neck

like a string of garlic.
this is the position for loving myself
I will die just once gnawing
the sober radish of the heart.

Queen of Heaven Mausoleum

white as coal-ash pressed
again in veins, fuel for the living
I lay all summer in the fourth

floor crypts chipping
the excess we poured in the footings
for the dead. the foreman kneels

to hand in the tools
his face framed by this inner
world square as an oven
in which my flesh warmed
death's inspired
ingredients. which was my hand
& which the dead hand wanting to pry
open the future, the concrete

forms a dead father reinforces
as he fills his son's
teetering flesh. after a moment
my eyes film, magnify
sparks dropping from the darkness
like snowflakes. I fall
back into the frozen position

of the dead or the foetus I once saw
in the clear icy jacket of a jar.
around my ankles something tightens
& pulls my legs straight
in this second more awkward birth
when the grinning foreman slaps
me from my faint, will I cry

to be buried or gratefully begin
to nurse at the world I thirsted for?

First Snow

for Ron Kritter

in all the feats of the snow there is not
one speckled egg
everyone uncovers his head
the bedding is washed: the last desperate crow
thrashes in its thickets
on the lines the sheets snap
dreaming of reins . . .
before this the urine was the only passage to the earth
before this all the alleys examined
the pearls of spit
the curbs gave up their last feathers to the vagrants
the shoeless dead
now the beautiful widow steps onto her porch
high up under the eaves . . . sends a moan through
the pulleys

California

The California Phrasebook

west of the Sierras where
the central valley
drifts on its crusts of almond
orchards the fields
die in a holiday accident
the freeways snapping
back in the dust like severed
arteries while the accomplished
doctor of silence stitches the evening
closed with stoplights which
never hold. gardens go
on their knees to the sun
all summer turning
over the brief counterfeit the rain
leaves, looking for a real
coin. in the arbors the Italian
uncles sit stirring anise-flavored
coffees, red bandanas
over their knees pulsing
with the sweating
body's rhythm like an open
chest in which the transplanted
organ of the homeland has not yet
begun to function.

in East Bay beyond the valley
towns pore to pore
the children black & brown
press out a test pattern
of veins, their faces rigid with long
division. they stand
in front of the blackboards looking
for their features, refusing
to draw the white mark
of a dollarsign while the mayor
waits & all the examining
board of cops waits, the correction
texts trembling in their hands.
why must we repeat our lessons,
let us go. in the alleys we rehearse
the lonely patrol of hands
over each other's bodies.
if we unfold a woman's creases
we are afraid to read
the platitudes. the black
penis is the last piece
of the puzzle we put in place
before the streetlamps have slipped
away in the wet fingers of the April
night, before the pathways
through the asphalt gardens
disgorge the feathers of the black
angel.

you who arrive late
from some forgotten Kansas
laminated of wheat & the sweet

alfalfa wasted with incurable winter
take root in the familiar
flat valley where the only
winter is overweight with rain
again & again welling up in fallen
wet fruit an early unearned
bitterness like the bum who drowses
under the indelible azaleas scrawled
against the capitol's white
walls. his life too
is a fragrant perennial.
he is less foreign than you,
but you must learn his difficult
language full of inflections for another
self palpable as the stone in spoiled
fruit. another self! the cheap
foundations of love shift—
before you always built in the quake-
proof plains where small rivers
pillow their heads in poplar
roots & turn all night
in the drought's persistent
insomnia. the cellar was dirt
still alive with roots
from which your father cut
your life in rigid board walls
incredibly steady
on the rippling floor of yellow
grain. in California the cellarless
houses sway at the slightest
tremor.

For Elizabeth, 1949-1968, Shelter Cove, Calif.

1
here is where we let go
the anchor-rope, undo the thin nets of cotton,
nylon, wool which caught a full
awkward animal & brought her home heavier,

no longer careful of the face
she poured from mirrors & drained
as a final medicine

2
in the closet her infant clothes dissolve
in their nectars of sweat.
each day, bruised, the summer slips a little
from its stone. her half-blind father poor
half-season fisher for crab & the huge
abalone which cling to the underside
of rocks so tightly you need an iron
bar to break them free, your chilly
testicles swinging in the rubber-waders
like two undersea eyes or stones you rubbed
all your life for luck, looking for a son
through the vacant streets of the womb tapping
with a penis, unable to see.

3
and now what keys will open
the flesh & expose the rooms where a young
man should have slept? what one-
way doors devour the nights
she lost? I am only the poet, I am like
the skull of an animal the indians
kept which when alive
was skilled in speech & dead answers
for the dead the indian relatives. the shaman skins
away all except the tongue which the soul
enters. no one came out

of her, head-first, as if falling
for an instant like the listener at a door
caught, as it opens to the father,
ashamed, being naked
to his own older image, having heard the dead
speak in his tongue: Elizabeth, having
no son, an older wishful one speaks
of the sharp key Death works like a knife
through the strange scrimshaw of all
our bones, the new brilliant beasts white
as snow we must become forsaking warm suits
of flesh to be gods of frost in this failing
California sun.

Bathing in Dead Man Creek

for George Keithley

I wake in another
skin, healed, having thrown
off all I had forgotten
I carried: what genetic chains
or weight the eyes gain
as they gather the loose change
of my life. what series of wombs
assembles us from the glazed

tide-pool shells & crawly
animals many winters ate
when glaciers pressed the dead
from their bodies & the soul remained

a fossilized handprint on the placenta.
this stream comes back
again this year having handled
roots & grazed in road-beds
till it assumes the currents & grain
of every living thing the seasons

put their hands to.

Poke-Pole Fishing

at minus tide the music
is deeper, gruff
music the retreating
sea makes in the rocks callused

with mussels you break
open for bait. the short
cuttyhunk bobs with its weight

on the limber twelve-
foot pole you poke in odd
sockets where eels
hold, tail in, to try whatever
the eclectic waves wash
through them. this music,
what more can you
catch, guess at, gummed down
by your small ration

of sense-news?
the pole is a parallel
to the horizon you lose as the opposite
earth pulls land from sea in fresh
creation. what custodian

fish will touch this index of another
world? you cannot reach the sea
by any step backward rigged

in clothes. the blenny eels imitate
kelp in its dwindling
from the land's foster-life.
tenant body, you too rehearse your
constituent parts, your intervals

of utter jubilee

Candlefish

indians used to burn their greasy
bodies for light
but the townsfolk simply fertilize
gardens with the chopped-up
fish & grow famous artichokes

hip-deep in the Eel saturday-night
fishermen dipnet whole constellations

while the wives of the absent professional
portugee seiners pinched
by metal buttons on their union
suits, scapulars climbing
the moist pucker between
their breasts eat mounds of fish

Monstrous Pictures of Whales

—the skeleton of a whale on the beach
near the mouth of a small river—

" . . . *the mere skeleton of the whale bears the same relation
to the fully-vested and padded animal as the insect does to
the chrysalis that so roundly envelops it.*"—*Melville*

I
   habits:
false. shoals.
& our hearts float

in the precious
oil. deep
in our heads the quiescent

   we were
before our illness:
mammals. ambergris

vestigial penis
perhaps
you & I identify

the long withdrawal: when
             the soft
edges wash & the stones

come clean

2
a jeep was stopped

inside
the skull. white

cormorants wobbled
their great

wings shaken
empty:

between the
ribs, turned sharply

into the windshield

3
with this map

I have left my house
with this skin wavering

over its own blue paths
the river
below is a direct turning
from the dryness
the mountains that nest

in the brown
forests, burns, sinks,
subtle switchbacks that go

nowhere. once
everyone went by boat.
Foster's Finger Gap.
heat
lightning chokes the
passes. the blood
descends

describing the possible
journeys. to this shore
the river comes
for the sake of the flesh

we follow it

4
a) one may drown in a windowpane

b) we may be seen floating white
   & wrinkled in our own eye

5
       in the center

the self turns
within currents the other

turns. try
to come back to the smallest
pool first. find straws
feeding

       till they
sink in rain-
pools. perhaps the river

failing
here. the whale half-
fish crushing
       the crowns of dune-
grass & the restless

bones at last
dig through fat & foreign
stones, flash

white out of the surfeit

Geography

Geography

the man away from home
has memorized his wife's
slip, charts his journey with a mental
ruler across her
chest, the sleepless islands.
sometimes with a small boy's
geography he can't
rough out where he loves
her & is lost
around her navel sunk
in sweat like a tide-pool.
he pictures his tongue
squirming, heavy
fish finding a way to gasp
out love as taste shrinks
this last water.
from a case of samples
he takes a lipstick
to plan a local version
of her body
as big as the motel bed.
on it he thrashes all night
misinformed by the old maps.

Building Marriage

consider the woods a rough
draft for towns: draw
a body, its uncertain
sex a shed of raw boards—

the rest, wild
orchard you bought of the literal
self. draw a face

doubled in the faulted groin
the shack fills—
house or stable the forfeited

animal self strokes
smooth with his tongue implying
speech. the roof if it reflects as a sky

should, mutual destiny,
dictates the rest.
from the unfinished window look

out on death laboring
the other side of the hill
his plow following the old horse-path

while inside, love like foal's breath
darkens the metal
pail from which it hesitantly
eats.

Self-Portrait

photos, survival maps to the past.
panic spooled on the brain
uncut, the negatives scaring
you with white hair or teeth blackened

with age. your bite fans
out as your image multiplies
whenever you stoop to drink

your face from the surface.
if it only would rain
the low places fill with tricky
currents to forget where boyhood ran
or what fish rose to indigenous

chum & debris you too
ate: bogus heroines forever
dead in sunk Buicks whose seats
you creased with love-maps.
the eyes are the first thing fish go for,
the lens inverts the life you really saw

Allergy

after the hospital
when she wakes her forehead
takes the matrix
of the field: that wind

fraying the odor
of clover & the soft-nosed
mole mending a new

hem her damp hair
makes across the face inlaid
with fever. her fingernails
are burnished with surface

blood: she is all gold with a rare
allergy common bees bring
redesigning in the honey-
comb of pores a delayed sweetness
even her husband cannot

trace, no matter
how much he thumps her flesh
into a lumpy bed for his
body or on her body draws other

maps of pain with a drunken
whipping. after all this she will

be home alone again
her graceful body rising
in small containers, windows,
mirrors as she passes

from one small job to another.

Tattoo Artist

I'm the one who corrects the blurred
bodies, those grown uneven,
out of focus with
   loneliness or if mates
overlap—here a Noah's
   pair, there a hoax of incoherent

parts taught life. if you prefer
   some peculiar
blemish to attract
her love, I'll make a blue
   kiss nest in the hairy

armpit, or trace a little
   cupid like summer love's last
fly alighting
   on a nipple, transpose

rudely done initials
   where a heart should
be. I can copy on your own
body whoever you really
   want: on your front her back

two-dimensional.
her sex arranged around yours—
    you can put your pants on over
all four legs. no one will
know when you lean
    against her in the sub-

way, or at night submit
    both of you to careful
pleasure. in the mirror you'll relish
    the outline of her
buttocks on you
as you move but never
    see her face tattooed face

down on yours.

Widow

in the burned-off Nevada
day the first
        star is the root
end of night. all the concentrated
        towns dissolve
in neon: casinos & wedding
chapels add the coupled

pulses. what am I worth
        wrapped only in my bedtime
prayers, the birthmark
or different lover's bite

like a canceled kiss insomnia
stamps on the body I wished
        to send to the one
I truly loved? this is my last
address—even the imago

divorcees' postdated faces
        shimmer a brief six
weeks in the bar glasses while
        my face is barely
intact in the egg-

sac of love-souvenirs.

The Name of Our Country

"Our Generall called this Countrey Nova Albion . . . because it might have some affinitie with our Countrey in name, which sometimes was so called."—Hakluyt's Voyages

I
islands move inward
water-marked where the weathers
   unravel each level
till the true face shakes
   free & the islander aware
incredibly treads
   water. the ranger at Point
Reyes told the legend of Drake's
landing. how the cliffs that fall
   away a little every year
recalled the island home whose

wasting body Drake bore
in the liquid isolation where his own
   body fought the surface, eyes
shut that he might not spill
   a dissolving image. no one
drowns at first though the heart

fills with a weightless
    swaying & we are ready to turn
away the breath that crouches
like a wet animal
    in the mouth, preferring
for a moment the forms the moisture
    takes as it floats the coiled
insides that once worked

with their own currents.
a year's voyage looking back
    on a clear day from these cliffs
to the fog-bound Farallones
twenty-four miles distant though
a part of the present coast
    solid to the ocean
floor cleaned of whatever the waves
could carry away & later
    into another country throw

up suspended particles.

2

we came here for repairs
only. the long kiss of rust
   in the anchor-chains & cabin
metals, even mugs our lips print
   with tarnished love.
alone with what we live by,
   wedded to breath-
soaked wreckage, two-thirds water
we wander finger & arm
   into our flesh, land

in a seven-day world
its roof of birds & daily walls
   dividing our lives dried of sleep
as a sailor's dream. the first
   day we dig oysters, drag
stores up the estuary & pray

God dress the dilated
   solitude with proper beasts
tame as the breath we draw
in threads through this foreign
   tapestry. a devoted summer has closed

the ditches with bindweed & mends
   the crumpled bottomland
with bits of color. our melancholy
carpenter in tears trims firs
   for spars tries to memorize
the countersign this lands leaves
   in the drooling rings.

3
seals & indians suffer
   go wounded with the lost
harpoon scanning the dark skins
for the direction of the blood
   & the bones that move
out like sandbars in the shallow
waves of the skull:
   how long since the great

white gods landed & we
   listened unable to think what
we called ourselves. who blended
us soft as curd in the quivering
   pouch of the mother,

made the seal dog for our drowned
   brother, out of breath
& unable to hunt for himself.
how can we reply—your voice breaks
   off in our mouths when we repeat
your questions. flickering palm

is the sign for seal or fish,
for man our hands are crippled
   with heavy secrets.
if we answer it will be with our eyes
   drifting like jellyfish
on the death-swell, self-stung
   for what they saw.

4
a cupful to drink
from the uncovered eye. not the ocean
    its small solids that drain
away to the bottom when the memory
    bends to taste nor English

marshes weighed in place
with winter fogs & rank blooms
    suffocating the sheep-folds
lip to lip over the laths
    too much alive like tumors:
what can we pray to

who have evolved in this voyage
from the flesh & can't follow Drake
    in his despair spreading
spare canvas every night to catch
    dew when his new casks split
like saints' bodies with that excess
    of another world. every day

the wind unravels
land-smells from the sailor's
    nose until the lungs are caught
paired ancient animals the shut
    Ark of his skull forced
to swim. the sea is our new country
& the senses crawl slowly
    over the surface not heavy
enough to sink.